THE
HISPANIC QUESTION COLL

**MORE THAN 200 QUESTIONS ABOUT HISTORY, GEOGRAPHY, CUSTOMS,
HOLIDAYS & CELEBRATIONS, SPORTS & GAMES, FOOD, AND MORE**

Written by Diane Sylvester • Illustrated by Celina R. Paredes

The Learning Works

Text Design and Editorial Production: Sherri M. Butterfield
Typesetting: Clark Editorial & Design

Copyright © 1994
THE LEARNING WORKS, INC.
P.O. Box 6187
Santa Barbara, CA 93160
All rights reserved.
Printed in the United States of America.

Library of Congress Number: 94-077365
ISBN: 0-88160-263-9

Introduction

This book is a collection of more than 200 questions on Latin America with specific questions about the Hispanic countries of Argentina, Belize, the Bahamas, Bolivia, Brazil, Chile, Colombia, Cuba, Ecuador, El Salvador, Grenada, Guatemala, Haiti, Honduras, Jamaica, Martinique, Mexico, Nicaragua, Panama, Paraguay, Peru, Puerto Rico, Suriname, and Venezuela.

The questions cover a variety of topics, including food, clothing, language, customs, history and heroes, holidays and celebrations, sports and games, religions and rituals, arts and crafts, geography, places of interest, and more. These questions are intended for use in the classroom, at home, or anywhere that children have empty minutes to fill, and are ideal for keeping kids occupied on rainy days, before recess, or while traveling.

The Hispanic Question Collection
© 1994—The Learning Works, Inc.

Introduction
(continued)

    The questions have been placed two to a page. While an effort has been made to vary both the countries and the topics across a two-page spread, the arrangement of these questions is random. Thus, they can be asked and answered in any order.

    No collection of questions would be complete without a collection of answers. For this book, the answers appear on pages 109–119. These answers have been listed by page number and keyed by letter to a particular position on the page. Thus, answer **a** is for the question on the left side of the page, and answer **b** is for the question on the right side of the page. See diagram.

a	b

A Special Message to Teachers

The ways to use this book in your classroom are almost endless. To begin with, of course, you can open it to any page and ask a few questions to fill those last few restless minutes before lunch or recess.

You can turn the questions into a self-checking game. Select pages on which the questions are appropriate for the grade level you teach. Duplicate some of these pages, and cut the questions apart. Glue each question to one side of a plain index card. Glue or write the corresponding answer on the other side of the card. Laminate the cards and make them available as part of a classroom display or learning center.

You can turn the process of answering the questions into a research activity. Select pages on which the questions are somewhat challenging for the grade level you teach. Duplicate these pages and make cards but do not write the answers on the cards. Instead, write the corresponding page number and the answer letter (that is, a or b).

The Hispanic Question Collection
© 1994—The Learning Works, Inc.

A Special Message to Teachers
(continued)

Distribute the cards, and challenge individual students or teams to find and record the answers within some specified period of time. Then, check their results against the answer key. You may want to keep score on a chart or graph by week or month.

Use the question cards to play Hispanic Answers Tic-Tac-Toe. With ribbon or yarn, make a large tic-tac-toe grid on your multicultural bulletin board. Place one question card in each of the nine squares on the grid. Challenge your students—working alone or in teams—to find the answers to any three questions that will give them three in a row horizontally, vertically, or diagonally.

You can use questions on a particular topic as part of a classroom display on that topic. Look through the book and select a group of questions that are related by topic.

A Special Message to Teachers
(continued)

For example, you might select questions about a specific country or about the history, heroes, or holidays of the entire region. Duplicate the pages on which these questions appear. Cut out the questions you have selected and post them on a classroom bulletin board or wall. Make blank cards available, and suggest that students write and illustrate additional questions about the same topic and add them to the display.

In addition, you can use these questions for question bees, for staged classroom quiz shows that follow a radio or television format, and as challenging bonus activities for students who have completed their assignments and are looking for something more to do. In short, you may find that this Hispanic question collection provides a lot of answers for a busy teacher with a bustling classroom.

The Hispanic Question Collection
© 1994—The Learning Works, Inc.

A Special Message to Parents

The ways to use this book are almost endless. It's perfect for increasing multicultural awareness, filling indoor time on rainy days, amusing a child who is ill, or making the miles go faster when you travel. For example, your child might use the questions it contains to stage a quiz show in radio or television format. For a change, let your child be the quiz master while you play contestant and try to supply the answers.

Use selected questions as a party game. Choose teams, ask questions, keep score, and reward the winners with prizes of some kind. Use this book to sharpen research skills. If your child does not know an answer, instead of revealing it, help him or her look it up in a dictionary, encyclopedia, or other similar reference book. You can also use this book as the inspiration for an art activity. Supply plain index cards and a black felt-tipped marking pen, and encourage your child to add to this Hispanic question collection.

What name is given
to a festive container
made of clay or cardboard,
decorated with colored paper,
filled with candy and toys,
and broken during celebrations?

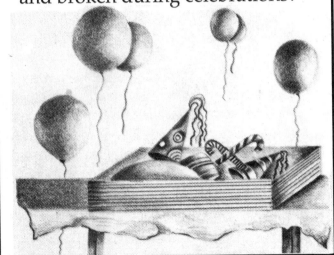

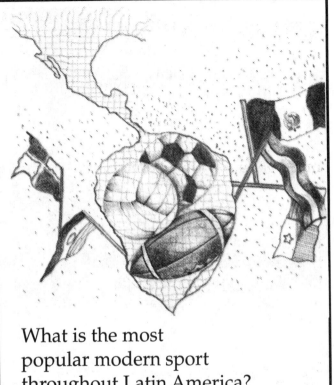

What is the most
popular modern sport
throughout Latin America?

9

The Hispanic Question Collection
© 1994—The Learning Works, Inc.

The longest mountain range
in the world is found
in South America.
What are the mountains
in this range called?

Guacamole is often served
south of the border.
What is the main ingredient
in this popular Mexican dish?

Is a *siesta*
an afternoon nap,
a desert plant,
a rare bird, or
a religious festival?

The largest
Portuguese-speaking
country in the world
is located in South America.
Name this country.

11

The Hispanic Question Collection
© 1994—The Learning Works, Inc.

The *capybara* is
a South American animal.
Is this animal
a bird, an insect,
a reptile, or a rodent?

What do archaeologists
call the basic unit
in the Aztec and Maya
system of writing?

The cities of
Acapulco, Juarez,
and Tijuana are found
in which Latin American country?

Is a *sarape* a Mexican crêpe,
a colorful blanket, a fragrant flower,
or an outdoor theater?

The Hispanic Question Collection
© 1994—The Learning Works, Inc.

The heaviest species of snake
in the world is found
in South America.
Snakes of this kind often weigh
more than 500 pounds.
Name this enormous snake.

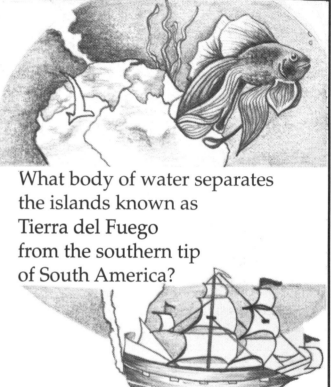

What body of water separates
the islands known as
Tierra del Fuego
from the southern tip
of South America?

Is Pelé the name
of an Andean mountain,
a Brazilian soccer player,
a South American city,
or a tropical fruit?

The longest and narrowest
country in the world
is found in South America.
Name this country.

The Hispanic Question Collection
© 1994—The Learning Works, Inc.

What name is given to the high-crowned, large-brimmed hat, made of felt or straw, which is worn in the southwestern United States and in Mexico?

Bogotá is the capital of which South American country?

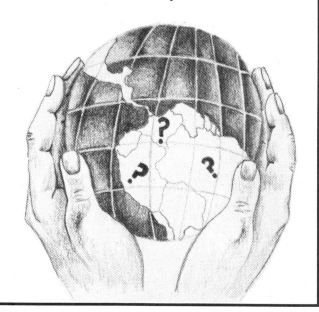

Flan is popular in Mexico.
Is it a fancy hat,
a fast dance, or
a custard dessert?

Copacabana and Ipanema
are both located
in Río de Janeiro, Brazil.
What are they?

The Hispanic Question Collection
© 1994—The Learning Works, Inc.

Which of these words, frequently used in the United States, did **not** come from Mexico: canyon, patio, pencil, or rodeo?

Which South American country lies directly north of Bolivia?

The longest
South American river
is also the world's
largest waterway.
Name this river.

Machu Picchu is in Peru.
Is it an active volcano,
a long river, or the site
of an ancient Inca city?

19

What name is given to the sun-dried clay which has been is used as a building material in Mexico for centuries?

The Panama Canal, located in Central America, connects which two oceans?

What name is given
to the public square
that is the center of life
in many Mexican towns?

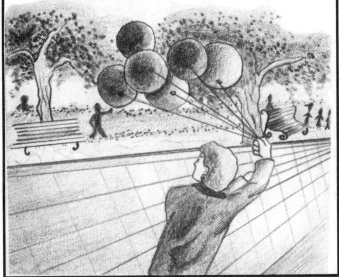

Jalapeños are an ingredient
in many Mexican foods.
Are they cheeses,
coffee beans, corn kernels,
or green peppers?

21

What name is given to a lace cloth worn over the head and shoulders by Latin American women?

Which Latin American country was the world's first black republic and is also the second oldest independent nation in the Americas?

If you visited a ranch in Chile, you might see a *huaso*. Would you be looking at a barn, a fence, a horseman, a rope, or a saddle?

Which one of these bodies of water does **not** border Mexico: the Atlantic Ocean, the Gulf of California, the Mediterranean Sea, or the Pacific Ocean?

23

In which South American city is the 11-story concrete statue of Christ the Redeemer found?

The largest tropical rain forest in the world is found in South America. What is the name of this forest?

Navidad is the Spanish name for which holiday: Christmas, Halloween, Independence Day, Thanksgiving, or Valentine's Day?

What is the name of the Jamaican dance in which dancers bend over backwards and pass under a pole?

The Hispanic Question Collection
© 1994—The Learning Works, Inc.

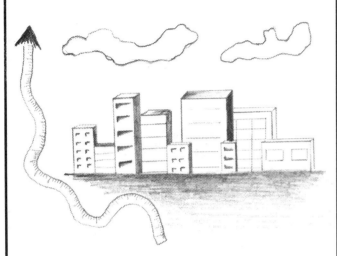

Situated nearly 12,000 feet above sea level, La Paz is the highest capital in the world. In which South American country would you find this city?

What is the Spanish word for a thin, round pancake, usually made from cornmeal?

Which two countries are located on the island of Hispaniola?

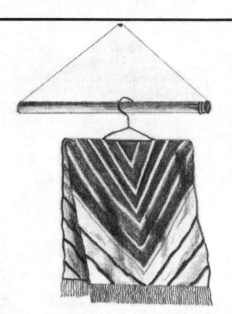

What Latin American garment is made from a blanket with a slit in the center for the wearer's head?

27

What is the basic
unit of money
in Mexico?

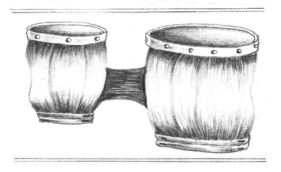

What musical instrument,
popular in Cuba,
consists of two tuned drums
bound together and
played with the hands?

Is a *mariachi*
a black hat,
a large guitar,
a wide leather belt, or
a Mexican street band?

Four hundred years ago,
large beans found growing near
the capitalof a South American
country were named after that city
Name the beans and the country.

The Hispanic Question Collection
© 1994—The Learning Works, Inc.

Which Latin American country is the smallest mainland nation in the Western hemisphere?

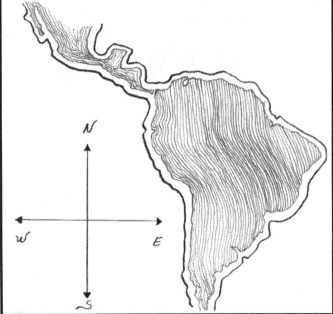

Are *huaraches* fried fish, folk songs, woven leather sandals, or violent storms?

What does
the Spanish word
chile mean?

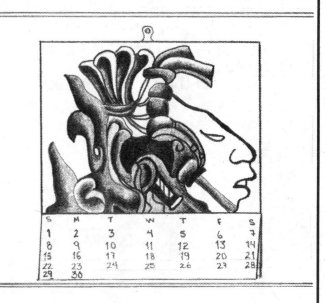

During which month is
Mexico's Independence Day
celebrated?

The Hispanic Question Collection
© 1994—The Learning Works, Inc.

Which river forms
about two-thirds
of the boundary between
Mexico and the United States?

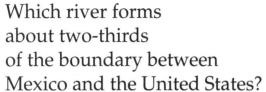

Are *frijoles* Mexican beans,
clothes, dances, or insects?

What color is *verde*?

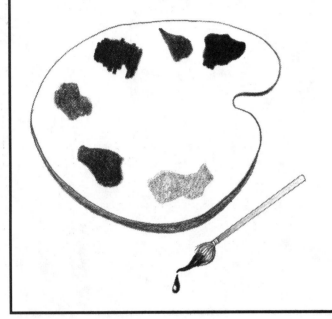

The southern tip
of South America
is less than half a mile
from which continent?

33

The Hispanic Question Collection
© 1994—The Learning Works, Inc.

What popular Mexican food consists of a folded tortilla filled with meat or cheese and covered with a spicy sauce?

What do people of Latin America call their religious and political festivals?

What Puerto Rican baseball player was elected to the Baseball Hall of Fame in 1973?

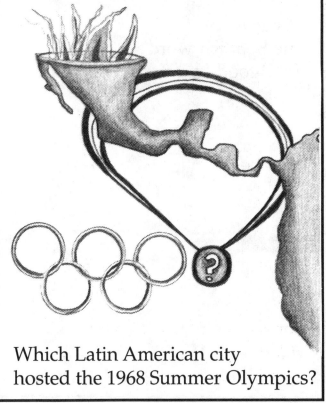

Which Latin American city hosted the 1968 Summer Olympics?

The Hispanic Question Collection
© 1994—The Learning Works, Inc.

What is
the Spanish word
for "good-bye"?

Which South American
country did the explorer
Amerigo Vespucci
name after the Italian city
of Venice?

Is a *hacienda*
a brick oven,
a country estate,
holiday dessert, or
a horse-drawn carriage?

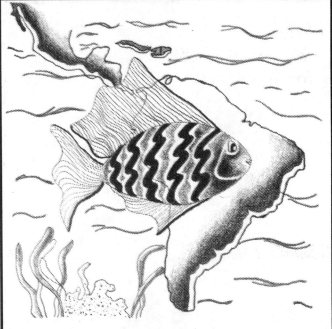

The island of Jamaica
is located in which sea?

The Hispanic Question Collection
© 1994—The Learning Works, Inc.

What is
the official language
of Haiti?

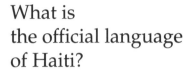

What name is given to the cowboys
who ride the plains of Argentina?

Rubber trees are grown
on plantations in South America.
What name is given
to the milky sap that comes
from these trees?

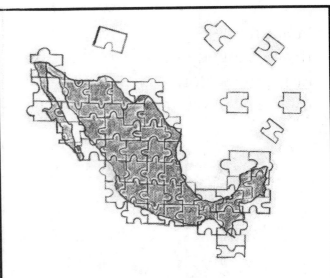

The country of Mexico
includes how many states?

The Hispanic Question Collection
© 1994—The Learning Works, Inc.

What name is given
to the fringed shawl
sometimes worn
by Mexican women?

The *pampas* are located
east of the Andes.
Are they adobe villages,
grass-covered plains,
or protected wetlands?

Argentina gets its name
from the Latin word *argentum*.
What does this word mean?

What name is given
to the holiday on which
the people of Mexico remember
the battle of Puebla and
a man named Benito Juárez?

The Hispanic Question Collection
© 1994—The Learning Works, Inc.

Which two animals are found on the flag of Mexico?

What is the capital of Chile?

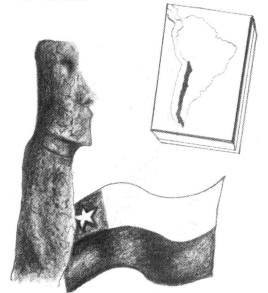

What Latin American percussion instruments are made from dried gourds and shaken to produce a rattling sound?

The Cayman Islands are named for an animal called a caiman. Is a *caiman* a bird, a mammal, or a reptile?

43

What is
the Spanish word
for Indian corn?

What is the
national sport
of Venezuela?

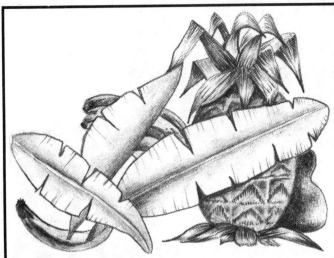

The ***plantain***
is a starchy food
often eaten in Puerto Rico
and other tropical countries.
Which common fruit
does it resemble?

Maracaña Stadium,
the world's largest
soccer facility,
is located in which
South American city?

45

The Hispanic Question Collection
© 1994—The Learning Works, Inc.

What popular food is made
from the beans
of the cacao tree?

What is the largest lake
in South America?

What is the name
of the highway that links
South American countries?

In which South American country
is the Atacama Desert located?

The Hispanic Question Collection
© 1994—The Learning Works, Inc.

Which of these vegetables
is **not** native to South America:
the lima bean, the carrot,
the potato, or the tomato?

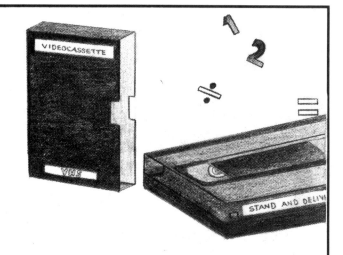

Name the Bolivian-born
mathematics educator
whose teaching methods
were the inspiration
for a feature film entitled
Stand and Deliver.

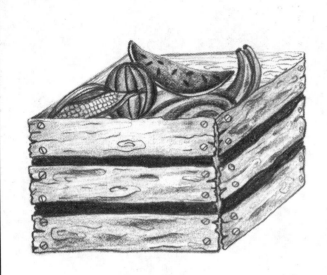

What is Ecuador's
most important
export crop?

Which Latin American country
is known as the
"crossroads of the world"?

The Hispanic Question Collection
© 1994—The Learning Works, Inc.

Which island,
off the coast of French Guiana,
was the site of a notorious prison?

Which disastrous act of nature
is named after Juracán,
the Arawak god of evil?

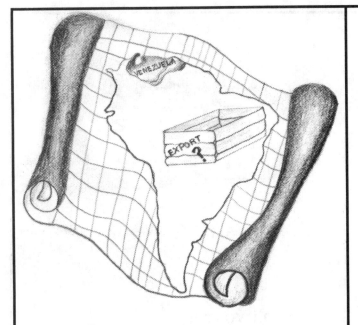

What natural resource is Venezuela's most valuable export?

Empanadas are a popular food in Chile. Are they hard candies, fresh vegetables, meat-filled turnovers, or dairy desserts?

51

The highest mountain
in the Andes and
in the Western Hemisphere
is located in Argentina.
What is the name
of this 22,834-foot peak?

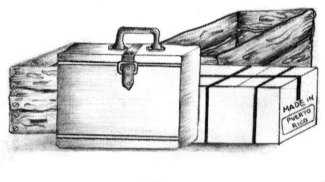

Which two crops
are Puerto Rico's
leading exports?

Which Central American country has the most volcanoes?

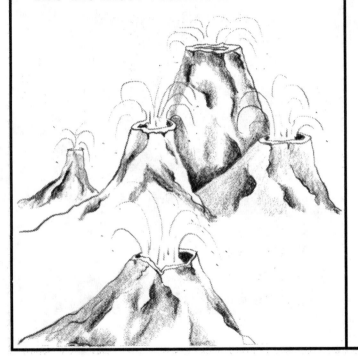

The Orinoco crocodile, one of the 12 most endangered species, makes its home in which South American country?

The Hispanic Question Collection
© 1994—The Learning Works, Inc.

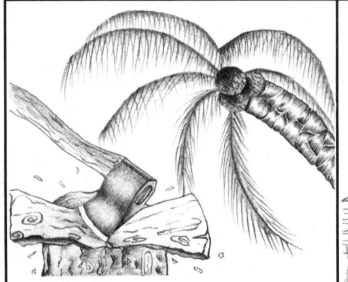

The carnauba palm
grows in Brazil.
What product is obtained
from the leaves of this tree?

Chan Chan is the largest
adobe city in the world.
Name the South American
country in which this
12-mile-long city is located.

Friendship Bridge,
the largest single-span
bridge in the world,
connects which two countries?

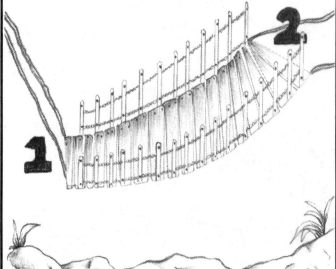

Is the Yucatán Peninsula
a part of Belize, Cuba,
Guatemala, or Mexico?

The Hispanic Question Collection
© 1994—The Learning Works, Inc.

What percentage of Panama is covered by dense jungle?

Which South American capital city is surrounded by volcanoes?

Is the largest
South American member
of the cat family a jaguar,
a puma, or a tiger?

What is the Spanish word
for the number two?

The Hispanic Question Collection
© 1994—The Learning Works, Inc.

Brazil shares its boundaries with all of the countries in South American except two. Name these two countries.

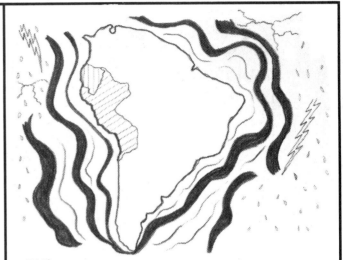

What name is given to the warm ocean current that develops along the coast of Ecuador and Peru and sometimes causes catastrophic weather conditions?

Which instrument is **not** usually found in a *mariachi*: an accordion, a guitar, a trumpet, or a violin?

What is the name of the South American soldier and statesman who liberated Venezuela?

LIBERTY

Venezuela

The Hispanic Question Collection
© 1994—The Learning Works, Inc.

What type of music—
originally from Trinidad—
is typically played
on steel drums?

What is the
national flower
of Panama?

What is the name
of the volcano on Martinque
which erupted in 1902
and killed more than
30,000 people?

What name is given
to the Central American
musical instrument
that is similar to
a xylophone?

The Hispanic Question Collection
© 1994—The Learning Works, Inc.

Is *masa*
corn dough,
a musical composition,
or a high plateau?

What is the name
of the courtyard
that serves as the
center of family life
in many Mexican homes?

What type of bean
was used as money
by the pre-Columbian
Indians of Mexico?

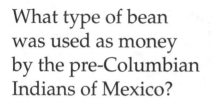

For what discovery
is Carlos Finlay,
a Cuban physician
and biologist,
famous?

Which country ranks
second in population
and third in area
among the nations
of Latin America?

Alpacas, llamas, and vicuñas—
grown at the higher altitudes
in Bolivia and Chile
for their milk, meat, and wool—
are members of which
animal family?

In which South American country was the world's highest standard-gauge railroad built?

Which Latin American country leads all others in sugar production?

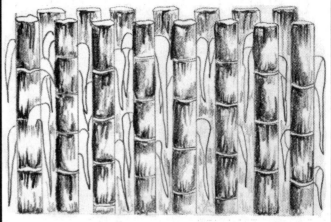

The Hispanic Question Collection
© 1994—The Learning Works, Inc.

In 1945,
Lucila Godoy Alcayaga
became the first
Latin American to receive
a Nobel Prize in literature.
Under what name did
this poet-educator write?

The Cuna Indians of Panama are famous for *mola* making, an art form they created. Is a mola made of cloth, pottery, or wood?

Of the 13 countries
on the continent
of South America,
which two are
landlocked?

What Argentinean
general and statesman
liberated Chile and
most of Peru
from Spain?

The Hispanic Question Collection
© 1994—The Learning Works, Inc.

Which city is the largest
in Mexico and serves
as that country's capital?

When an Argentinean gaucho uses
a **bola**, is he cooking, dancing
or hunting?

Name the river whose waters were dammed when the Panama Canal was built.

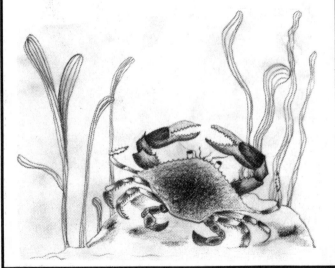

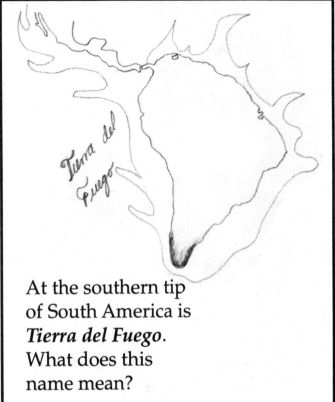

At the southern tip of South America is *Tierra del Fuego*. What does this name mean?

69

The Hispanic Question Collection
© 1994—The Learning Works, Inc.

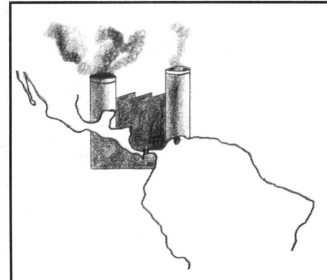

Which country
is the smallest,
most densely populated,
and most industrialized nation
in Central America?

Which one
of these countries
is **not** among the
leading coffee producers
in Latin America:
Brazil, Chile, Costa Rica,
or Guatemala?

Is *nandutí*—
made by the
Guaraní Indian
women of Paraguay—
decorated pottery,
fine lace, or woven cloth?

What name is given
to the great plains region
of Colombia and Venezuela?

71

The Hispanic Question Collection
© 1994—The Learning Works, Inc.

Which South American waterway is 1,370 miles long and ranks as the eighth longest river in the world?

Are cowboys who ride the great plains of Venezuela called *charros*, *gauchos*, *llaneros*, or *vaqueros*?

Which South American
waterfall consists of
275 cascades and
is two miles wide?

What is the name
of the city in Mexico
where the great pyramids
of the Sun and Moon
are located?

The Hispanic Question Collection
© 1994—The Learning Works, Inc.

What is the name
of the fast-paced ball game
in which players use
a basket-like racket to hurl
a ball against a wall?

What would
your occupation be
if you were
a *torero* or a *torera*?

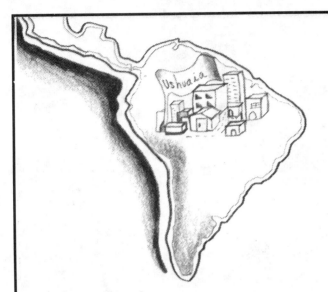

Ushuaia is the
southernmost town
in the world.
In which country
is this town located?

Who came to power
in Cuba in 1959 and
turned that country
into a communist
dictatorship?

The Hispanic Question Collection
© 1994—The Learning Works, Inc.

Which islands—located in
the Pacific Ocean near Ecuador—
were named for the giant tortoises
that inhabit them?

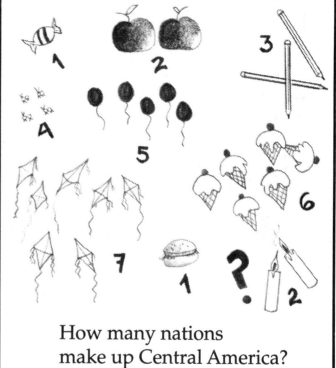

How many nations
make up Central America?

What is the name
of the lower tip
of South America,
which is known
for its stormy climate?

A *metate* is a large, smooth stone
with a concave surface.
Is it used for grinding corn,
scratching designs in pottery,
or sharpening knives?

Name the Chilean island that is the site of some 600 mysterious, carved stone figures dating back as far as A.D. 900.

The *mandioca* is a root native to Brazil. What starchy substance, sometimes used in puddings, is made from this plant?

Which Brazilian holiday celebration takes place immediately before Lent and features parades with floats and costumed dancers?

The world's highest known waterfall is found in Venezuela. What is the name of this 3,212-foot fall?

79

The Hispanic Question Collection
© 1994—The Learning Works, Inc.

Are Bossa Nova, Samba,
and Tango the names
of South American cities,
dances, foods, mountains,
rivers, or waterfalls?

The ancient settlers
of the Valley of Mexico
grew corn and other crops
in *chinampas*.
What English term describes
this agricultural technique?

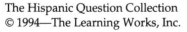

Which animal would **not** be found in a South American rain forest: a coati, a gorilla, a macaw, or an ocelot?

If you visited a *mercado* in Latin America, where would you be?

81

What is the color
of the unique pottery
that comes from
Oaxaca, Mexico?

What narrow isthmus
links the continents
of North America
and South America?

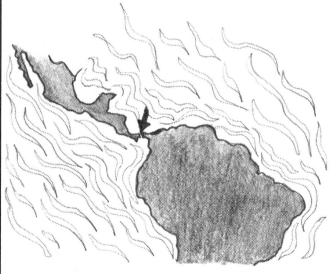

What is the largest
island in the West Indies?

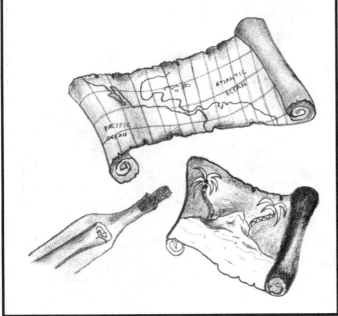

While in Bolivia,
if you enjoyed *chuño*,
would you be
eating processed potatoes,
sipping tea, taking a nap,
or watching a dance?

83

The Hispanic Question Collection
© 1994—The Learning Works, Inc.

The bark of which
South American tree
is the source of quinine,
a drug used to treat malaria?

Which Spanish explorer,
best known for his search
for the Fountain of Youth,
explored and colonized
Puerto Rico?

A famous children's story is about *tres osos*. What is the English title of this tale?

Miami, Florida, is on the Atlantic Ocean. Lima, Peru, is on the Pacific Ocean. Does Lima lie east or west of Miami?

The Hispanic Question Collection
© 1994—The Learning Works, Inc.

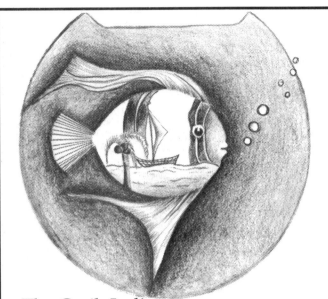

The Carib Indians moved into the West Indies between A.D. 1000 and 1500. What body of water is named after them?

Edward Teach was a pirate who sailed in the West Indies. By what other name was he known?

Salsa can be either a hot pepper sauce or a zesty type of Latin American music. Are the sounds of this music primarily American Indian, Afro-Caribbean, country-western, or hard rock?

Is a guitar made of armadillo shells called a *charango*, a *charro*, or a *chorizo*?

The Hispanic Question Collection
© 1994—The Learning Works, Inc.

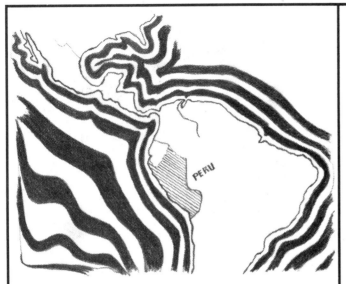

What is the name of the ancient Inca capital, which was located high in the Andes of Peru?

Jangadas are used by the fisherman of Brazil. Is a *jangada* a large net, a long line, or a light raft?

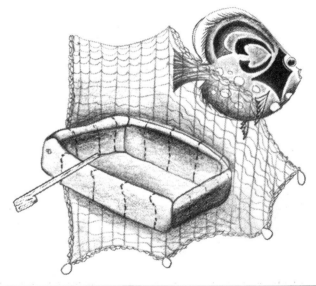

What is the name of the United States naval base located on the island of Cuba?

Are Mexican artists José Clemente Orozco, Diego Rivera, and David Alfaro Siqueiros famous for their mosaics, their murals, or their weavings?

What is the
most common food
in Argentina?

The basic unit of money
in modern Guatemala and
that country's national bird
share the same name.
What is it?

Maté is made from young holly leaves. Is this popular food a relish, a spice, or a tea?

What has been Puerto Rico's leading crop since the eighteenth century?

The Hispanic Question Collection
© 1994—The Learning Works, Inc.

Is the *coquí*
a Puerto Rican
fiesta, food, or frog?

The Olmecs, Zapotecs,
Mixtecs, and Toltecs
were ancient inhabitants
of which Latin American
country?

Renaissance Italy was famous for sculptures. For what art form is twentieth-century Mexico most famous?

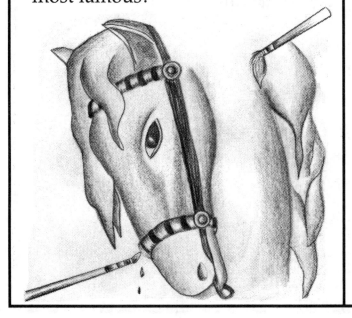

What modern city stands on the site of the ancient Aztec capital called Tenochtitlán?

The Hispanic Question Collection
© 1994—The Learning Works, Inc.

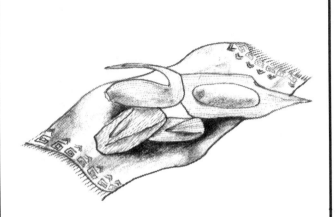

The **tamale** is a favorite Mexican food which consists of spicy beef, rolled in cornmeal, and wrapped in corn husks. What is this food called in Venezuela?

Costa Rica is a country in Central America. What does its Spanish name mean?

What South American bird has a wing span of nearly 10 feet?

Is a *cuatro*
an exotic bird,
a guitarlike instrument,
a straw hat, or
a woven basket.

The Hispanic Question Collection
© 1994—The Learning Works, Inc.

What ancient Maya city—located in Chiapas, Mexico—was named "painted walls" because of the murals found there?

What name is given to the Mexican horsemen who are famous for their riding and roping skills and for their colorful costumes?

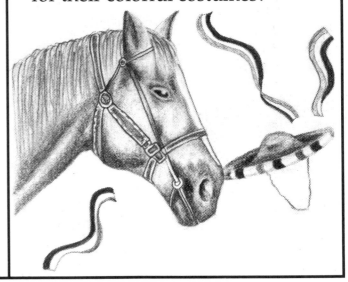

What is
the main religion
throughout Latin America?

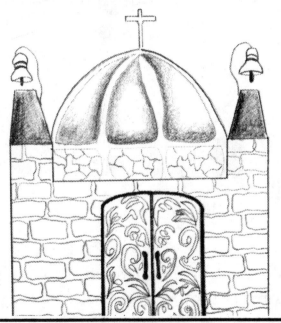

In which country would you find
these cities: Córdoba, Corrientes,
Resistencia, Rosario,
and Santa Rosa?

The Hispanic Question Collection
© 1994—The Learning Works, Inc.

Did the Aztecs consider
Quetzalcoatl to be
an amazing athlete,
a victorious general,
a wise ruler, or
a feathered serpent god.

What is the Spanish word
for the number eight?

What is the
second largest river
in South America?

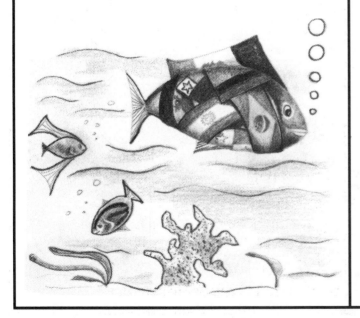

Because the Incas had
no written words or
numbers, they used
quipus to keep records.
What are **quipus**?

The Hispanic Question Collection
© 1994—The Learning Works, Inc.

Were the first
inhabitants of Puerto Rico
the Arawak Indians,
the Carib Indians,
the Inca, the Maya,
or the Spanish?

What is Tegucigalpa?

What ancient people of Peru built the world's first known suspension bridges—of braided fiber and vine cable—to span that country's ravines and conquer its deep chasms?

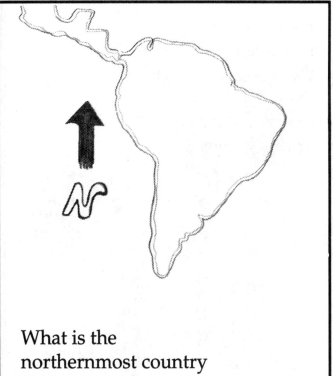

What is the northernmost country in Central America?

The Hispanic Question Collection
© 1994—The Learning Works, Inc.

Mexico gets its name
from a group of people
called the Mexica.
By what other name
is this group known?

What was Belize called
before 1981, when it won
independence from
Great Britain?

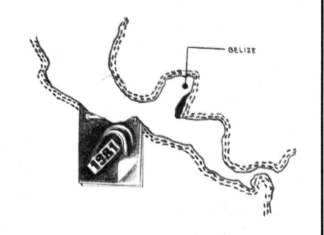

BELIZE

1981

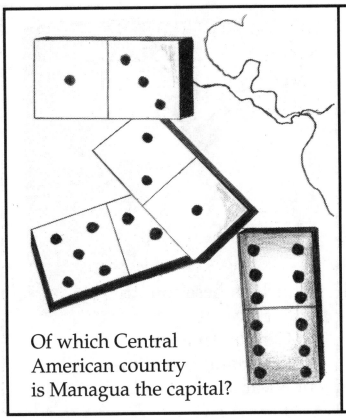

Of which Central American country is Managua the capital?

What nation lies east of Florida, includes 700 islands—22 of them inhabited—and attracts 1.7 million tourists each year?

The Hispanic Question Collection
© 1994—The Learning Works, Inc.

What Spanish word means a range of mountains with jagged or sawlike ridges?

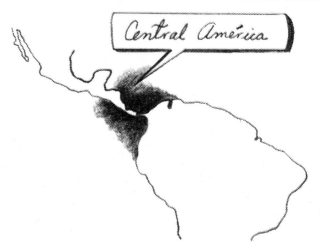

Which of these countries is **not** located in Central America: Belize, Haiti, Honduras, or Nicaragua?

What is
the official name
of Mexico?

What Latin American
religious symbol
consists of colored threads
wrapped in a special pattern
around crossed sticks?

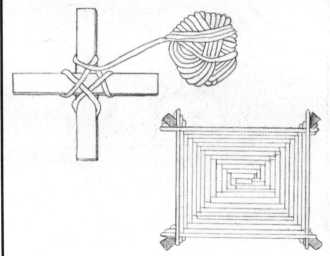

The Hispanic Question Collection
© 1994—The Learning Works, Inc.

What is the meaning
of the Spanish word
barrio?

For which ancient people
was Montezuma the emperor?

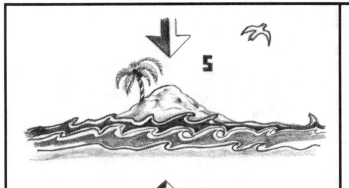

Which island joined with the southern isles of the Grenadines in 1974 to become the smallest independent nation in the Western Hemisphere?

The Spanish word *colorado* names a color. Which one?

The Hispanic Question Collection
© 1994—The Learning Works, Inc.

Which island
in the West Indies
is a self-governing
commonwealth
whose people are
citizens of the United States?

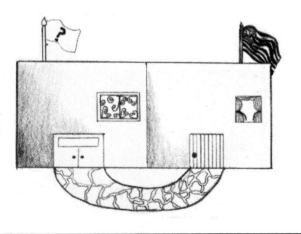

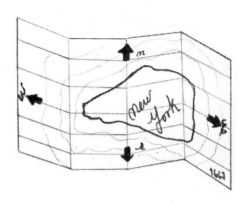

In 1667, England
gave a prosperous
South American colony
to Holland in exchange
for New York. What
is this colony called
today?

Answer Key

Page 9
a. *piñata*
b. soccer

Page 10
a. the Andes
b. avocado

Page 11
a. an afternoon nap
b. Brazil

Page 12
a. a rodent
b. a glyph

Page 13
a. Mexico
b. a colorful blanket

Page 14
a. the anaconda
b. the Strait of Magellan

Page 15
a. a Brazilian soccer player
b. Chile

Page 16
a. sombrero
b. Colombia

Page 17
a. a custard dessert
b. beaches

The Hispanic Question Collection
© 1994—The Learning Works, Inc.

Page 18
a. pencil
b. Brazil

Page 19
a. the Amazon River
b. the site of an ancient Incan city

Page 20
a. *adobe*
b. the Atlantic and the Pacific

Page 21
a. the plaza
b. green peppers

Page 22
a. *mantilla*
b. Haiti

Page 23
a. a horseman
b. the Mediterranean Sea

Page 24
a. Río de Janeiro, Brazil
b. the Amazonian rain forest

Page 25
a. Christmas
b. the limbo

Page 26
a. Bolivia
b. *tortilla*

Page 27
a. the Dominican Republic and Haiti
b. a poncho

Page 28
a. the peso
b. a *bongó*

Page 29
a. a Mexican street band
b. lima beans; Peru

Page 30
a. El Salvador
b. woven leather sandals

Page 31
a. pepper
b. September

Page 32
a. the Río Grande
b. beans

Page 33
a. green
b. Antarctica

Page 34
a. an *enchilada*
b. fiestas

Page 35
a. Roberto Clemente
b. Mexico City

The Hispanic Question Collection
© 1994—The Learning Works, Inc.

Page 36
a. *adios*
b. Venezuela

Page 37
a. a country estate
b. the Caribbean Sea

Page 38
a. French
b. *gauchos*

Page 39
a. latex
b. 31 states

Page 40
a. *rebozo*
b. grass-covered plains

Page 41
a. "silver"
b. Cinco de Mayo

Page 42
a. a serpent and an eagle
b. Santiago

Page 43
a. *maracas*
b. a reptile

Page 44
a. *maíz*
b. baseball

Page 45
a. the banana
b. Río de Janeiro, Brazil

Page 46
a. chocolate
b. Lake Maracaibo

Page 47
a. the Pan American Highway
b. Chile

Page 48
a. the carrot
b. Jaime Escalante

Page 49
a. bananas
b. Panama

Page 50
a. Devil's Island
b. the hurricane

Page 51
a. oil
b. meat-filled turnovers

Page 52
a. Mount Aconcagua
b. copper and sugarcane

Page 53
a. El Salvador
b. Venezuela

The Hispanic Question Collection
© 1994—The Learning Works, Inc.

Page 54
a. wax for polishes and varnishes
b. Peru

Page 55
a. Brazil and Paraguay
b. Mexico

Page 56
a. 70 percent
b. Quito, Ecuador

Page 57
a. a jaguar
b. *dos*

Page 58
a. Chile and Ecuador
b. El Niño

Page 59
a. an accordion
b. Simón Bolivar

Page 60
a. calypso
b. a white orchid

Page 61
a. Mount Pelée
b. marimba

Page 62
a. corn dough
b. the patio

Page 63
a. the cacao bean
b. the discovery that mos-
     quitoes carry yellow fever

Page 64
a. Mexico
b. the camel family

Page 65
a. Peru
b. Cuba

Page 66
a. Gabriela Mistral
b. cloth

Page 67
a. Bolivia and Paraguay
b. José de San Martín

Page 68
a. Mexico City
b. hunting

Page 69
a. the Chagres River
b. "land of fire"

Page 70
a. El Salvador
b. Chile

Page 71
a. fine lace
b. *llanos*

The Hispanic Question Collection
© 1994—The Learning Works, Inc.

Page 72
a. the Orinoco River
b. *llaneros*

Page 73
a. Iguaçu Falls
b. Teotihuacán

Page 74
a. jai alai
b. a bullfighter

Page 75
a. Argentina
b. Fidel Castro

Page 76
a. the Galápagos Islands
b. seven

Page 77
a. Cape Horn
b. grinding corn

Page 78
a. Easter Island
b. tapioca

Page 79
a. Carnaval
b. Angel Falls

Page 80
a. dances
b. "floating gardens"

Page 81
a. a gorilla
b. in a marketplace

Page 82
a. black
b. the Isthmus of Panama

Page 83
a. Cuba
b. eating processed potatoes

Page 84
a. the cinchona tree
b. Juan Ponce de León

Page 85
a. "The Three Bears"
b. east

Page 86
a. the Caribbean Sea
b. Blackbeard

Page 87
a. Afro-Caribbean
b. a *charango*

Page 88
a. Cuzco
b. a light raft

Page 89
a. Guantánamo
b. murals

The Hispanic Question Collection
© 1994—The Learning Works, Inc.

Page 90
a. beef
b. the quetzal

Page 91
a. a tea
b. sugarcane

Page 92
a. frog
b. Mexico

Page 93
a. murals
b. Mexico City

Page 94
a. a *hallaca*
b. "rich coast"

Page 95
a. the South American condor
b. a guitarlike instrument

Page 96
a. Bonampak
b. *charros*

Page 97
a. Roman Catholicism
b. Argentina

Page 98
a. a feathered serpent god
b. *ocho*

Page 99
a. the Río de la Plata
b. strands of knotted yarn

Page 100
a. the Arawak Indians
b. the capital of Honduras

Page 101
a. the Incas
b. Guatemala

Page 102
b. the Aztecs
b. British Honduras

Page 103
a. Nicaragua
b. the Bahamas

Page 104
a. *sierra*
b. Haiti

Page 105
a. *Los Estados Unidos Mexicanos*
b. the eye of god, or *Ojo de Dios*

Page 106
a. "neighborhood"
b. the Aztecs

Page 107
a. Grenada
b. red or ruddy

Page 108
a. Puerto Rico
b. Suriname

Celina R. Paredes was born in Guadalajara, Mexico, where she received her degree in painting from the Instituto Cultural Cabañas. Her artwork has been exhibited in various venues in Mexico, demonstrating her skill in water color, oils, and engravings. Celina's artistic skill and pride in her Hispanic heritage is reflected in the delicate pencil drawings found in *The Hispanic Question Collection*.